MW00478513

REIGN

Awakening a Young Generation to King Jesus

STUDENT BOOK

Richard Ross and Clayton Ross

For more information about Richard Ross, Clayton Ross, and Richard Ross Ministries, see RichardARoss.com. The mission of Richard Ross Ministries: By the Spirit, live, teach, speak, and write to see Christ's kingdom come through teenagers and their parents and leaders, for the glory of almighty God. Facebook.com/rossrichard. Twitter.com/richardaross

Reign: Awakening a Young Generation to King Jesus (Student Book)
By Richard Ross and Clayton Ross
Copyright © 2019 by Richard Ross

Editing by Judi Hayes
Front cover and interior design by Dave Wright (daveawright.com)
Back cover art by Steve Alberts (facebook.com/SteveAlbertsArtWorks)

ISBN-9781093482546

This resource is dedicated to David Bryant. Almost every thought in these pages can be traced back to David's writing and speaking. Beyond just thoughts, many of the phrases are his as well. David's seminal work has spread throughout the church and has shaped the thinking of multitudes.

David is the founder of Proclaim Hope!, a ministry that serves the church through a host of creative ministries designed to proclaim the full extent of Christ's supremacy and to empower others to do the same. Proclaimhope.com

David is author of many books, including his newest, *Christ Is Now!* David also is the driving force behind ChristNow.com. This website offers a one-of-a-kind, go-to hub of Christ-focused tools, training, e-books, blogs, podcasts, and videos, drawn from many streams of the church. Everything there is focused on exploring and experiencing a fresh vision of the supremacy of God's Son for the purpose of promoting a nationwide Christ awakening movement among God's people.

LITTLE JESUS IN MY POCKET

How True?

Children today grow up hearing: "Every child's a winner." "Everyone gets a trophy for participating." "Every child's the best." Even at church it's almost as if some adults told the children: "God is so lucky to have you. There He was, all lonely in heaven, with nothing much to do. Then you showed up on earth! Now He can think about you all the time. He sent Jesus to earth just to make you happier and happier. Since you're so special, Jesus exists for you."

I think this statement is about _____ percent true.

LITTLE JESUS

Distorted Views of Jesus

Place a 1 beside the distorted view of Jesus you're most likely to drift toward.

___ Jesus, the EMT
___ Jesus, the Santa Claus
___ Jesus, the Grandfather
___ Jesus, the Butler

An Affair with Jesus

A well-known worship leader once reported:

"Often it feels to me as if, for many of our people, singing praise songs and hymns on a Sunday morning has turned into an affair with Christ.

Many are far more passionate about worldly concerns such as getting ahead at school, finding personal happiness, driving a new car, or winning awards. But we rarely ever get that excited about Christ Himself.

"Except when we enter a sanctuary on a Sunday. Then for a while, we end up sort of 'swooning' over Christ with feel-good music and heart-stirring prayers—only to return to the daily grind of secular seductions to which we're thoroughly 'married.' Christ is more like a 'mistress' to us. He's someone with whom we have these periodic affairs to energize our spirits so we can return, refreshed, to those parts of our lives that are more important."

Jesus the Mascot

"Is Jesus our football mascot? On Sunday, do we 'trot Him out' to cheer us up and give us new energy? He lifts our spirits. He builds our confidence. He gives us reasons to cheer. We're so proud of Him!

"But each performance of our mascot is brief. Then He disappears, sent to the sidelines, and put on hold until the next setback. He has served his useful purpose. Everyone feels better now.

"Then, for the rest of the week, He is pretty much relegated to the sidelines as our figurehead. For all practical purposes, we are the ones who call the shots. We implement the plays, scramble for first downs, and improvise in a pinch.

"Our cheers may be for Him, but our victories are for us. We welcome Him to cheer us on and inspire our efforts. But in the end, the 'game' is really about us, not about Him. We have redefined Jesus into someone we can both admire and ignore at the same time! We've re-designed Him to be mostly out of sight, but 'on call' as needed."

Debate

Which of these two phrases is a better description of shallow believers?

"We're married to the world, but we just have an affair with Jesus."

"Jesus is our mascot, but that's about all."

Recent Prayers

Which of the following sounds more like your recent prayers?

_____ *"Jesus, Jesus, make everything in my life all better."*
_____ *"Mighty Christ, seated on the throne of heaven, you are my King forever. My life is completely in your hands and under your reign."*

MAJESTIC JESUS

Study a Bible Passage

Luke 24

Verse 50 _____ after His resurrection from the dead, Jesus led His followers to the _____.

Verse 51 Jesus rose from the Mount of Olives and went up _____.

Acts 1

Verses 1–2 until the day when he was taken up The day Jesus _____ into heaven.

Verse 3 He presented himself alive to them The _____ of Christ after He rose from the dead.

after his suffering Christ's _____ and all that led up to it.

appearing to them during forty days The period from the _____ to the ascension lasted forty days.

Verse 9 he was lifted up, and a cloud took him out of their sight Jesus ascended from the Mount of Olives, until He went up through the _____.

Verse 10 two men stood by them in white robes Two _____.

Verse 11 This Jesus, who was taken up from you into heaven, will come in the same way as you saw him go into heaven The angels announced that Jesus would return _____ in His second coming.

Psalm 110

_____ is the Old Testament passage most quoted by New Testament writers.

David wrote this psalm about a thousand years before Christ ascended.

After Jesus ascended from the Mount of Olives, He returned to _____. There He appeared before God the Father. God the Father then made a powerful statement to God the Son.

***Verse 1* The Lord says to my Lord: "Sit at my right hand** The Father told the Son to be seated on the right-hand throne.

The throne on the right represents honor, respect, and _____. Many Bible scholars believe the Father placed the Son on the right-hand throne so our attention would be riveted on Christ as the clearest revelation of the Godhead.

From that day until today, Christ has been reigning King of kings and Lord of lords!

until I make your enemies a footstool In that day kings sometimes demonstrated their complete domination over an enemy by putting their foot on his neck. God the Father promised His Son that He would bring all the forces of evil under such _____.

***Verse 2* The Lord sends forth from Zion your mighty scepter** The scepter is a symbol of Christ's current rule and _____ from heaven.

Rule in the midst of your enemies! Jesus reigns _____ heaven but also _____ heaven. He is Ruler over those who adore Him, and He is Ruler over those who hate Him. At the end of time, His _____ rule will be clear to all as every knee bows before Him.

Act It Out

A paraphrase of God the Father speaking to God the Son:

All You have accomplished for My people by Your incarnation,
Your life of righteousness, Your teachings and healings,

Your atoning sacrifice, and Your definitive disabling of death
are totally sufficient!
You have fulfilled all that's needed for the reclamation of the universe.
So come, My Son, take the crown and the glory;
begin to reign as King of kings and Lord of lords, forever and ever!

1 Thessalonians 4

Verse 16 **For the Lord himself will descend from heaven with a cry of command** The Greek word for **cry of command** refers to a _____ . Jesus will return as a victorious King, giving the word of command to the hosts of heaven at His final triumph over sin, death, and Satan.

with the sound of the trumpet In Scripture the trumpet often accompanies appearances of _____ .

Verse 17 **caught up together with them in the clouds** After the resurrection Christ ascended in the _____ . In His return He will descend in the _____ . The dead in Christ will return with Him in the _____ , and the believers alive at that time will rise to meet Him in the _____ .

The Second Coming

Imagine at this moment that your house begins to shake. Brilliant light floods in every window. You hear trumpet blasts ten times louder than any stereo. You and all the neighbors run outside and lift your eyes.

At that moment you see Christ split open the heavens. He begins slowly to descend to earth. Thousands of angels suddenly fill the sky and begin to sing praise to Him. The sights and sounds are overwhelming, and your emotions are a jumble of indescribable joy, awe, and a little fear.

Powerful Thought

Who Christ will be at His second coming is precisely who He is today.

MASCOT OR MONARCH

Mascot or Monarch?

If I believe Jesus mostly exists for me, I'm worshipping a mascot.
If I believe I exist for the glory of King Jesus, I'm worshipping a Monarch.

If I sit on the throne of my own life, I'm worshipping a mascot.
If I adore King Jesus as He reigns over my life, I'm worshipping a Monarch.

If I can *only* think of Jesus as He was in the flesh, I'm worshipping a mascot.
If I can think of Jesus as He was in the flesh *and* His burning holiness and unapproachable majesty on the throne of heaven, I'm worshipping a Monarch.

If I almost never speak of the power, greatness, and majesty of God's Son, I'm worshipping a mascot.
If I often speak of the power, greatness, and majesty of King Jesus, I'm worshipping a Monarch.

Where I Stand

I believe Jesus is a nice friend. He mostly lets me do whatever I want. He stays out of my way until I get in a jam. Then He shows up to fix things and make my life happier.
Or
I believe Jesus is God and thus is more powerful and glorious than anyone can know. He is the absolute King and Ruler over my life. He does not exist primarily for me. I exist completely for Him.

King Jesus Glasses

What are some elements of the Christian life that look differently if viewed through the lens of the greatness of God's Son?

Meeting Jesus . . . Again

Christian leader David Bryant reports this experience:

"Like John, I saw Jesus as I had never seen him before! I felt as though the Father *reintroduced* me to his Son, as if—what shall I say?—as if in some unexplainable way I was meeting Jesus again . . . for the first time! Sort of like I was being born again . . . *again*!"

Could you be approaching a similar moment in your life?

WHO JESUS IS TODAY

Student Readers

Reader 1: Jesus Christ has had three waves of glory. First, Jesus had glory as the Son of God before He came to earth and even before creation. In John 17:5, Jesus said, "And now, Father, glorify me in your own presence with the glory that I had with you before the world existed."

Reader 2: Second, Jesus had glory as God in the flesh during His days on earth. John said, "And the Word became flesh and dwelt among us, and we have seen his glory, glory as of the only Son from the Father, full of grace and truth" (John 1:14).

Reader 3: Third, Jesus today has glory as the exalted Son of God, after the resurrection and ascension. This session will consider all three waves of Christ's glory but give special attention to the third wave—who King Jesus is today.

JESUS IN THE BEGINNING

Study a Bible Passage

`John 1`

Verse 1 The word **beginning** refers to the first person or thing in a _____. That period before the world was. **Word** means _____.

and the Word was with God Jesus had an _____ distinct from God the Father but was inseparable from Him.

and the Word was God Jesus was and is _____.

Verse 2 **in the beginning with God** The period before _____, before time began

Study a Bible Passage

John 1

Verse 3 **All things were made through him** God made the world by a word, and _____ was the Word.

and without him was not any thing made that was made All _____ and _____ came into existence by Christ's command.

Study a Bible Passage

Colossians 1

Verse 15 **He is the image of the invisible God** God the Son became a man and thus became _____ to mankind.

the firstborn of all creation Jesus is preeminent over all _____.

Verse 16 **all things were created through him and for him**. Not only did God the Son create all things, but all things _____ for Him.

True or False

Mark the following True or False:

_____ All creation exists for Christ.

_____ Christ exists for all creation.

_____ Christ exists for me.

_____ I exist for Christ.

_____ Life is all about Christ.

_____ Life is all about me.

Study a Bible Passage

Colossians 1

Verse 17 **in him all things hold together**. Right now Jesus sustains everything by the _____ of His mind.

THE OLD TESTAMENT AND JESUS

Study a Bible Passage

Daniel 7

Verse 13 **behold** Daniel's way of saying that he is about to announce something _____.

son of man This phrase refers to the _____.

and he came to the Ancient of Days and was presented before him Christ was presented before God the Father.

Verse 14 **And to him was given dominion and glory and a kingdom** Christ was enthroned in heaven and absolutely _____ today.

that all peoples, nations, and languages should serve him Right now the Holy Spirit is calling and empowering believers to take the good news to the last _____.

his dominion is an everlasting dominion The kingdom of Christ will be _____.

JESUS AND THE NEW TESTAMENT

Study a Bible Passage

Luke 1

Verse 31 **you will conceive . . . and you shall call his name Jesus.** An angel announced to Mary that her baby would be _____ by the Holy Spirit and not by a human father (Luke 1:35).

Verses 32–33 **He will be great . . . called the Son of the Most High . . . the throne . . . he will reign . . . of his kingdom there will be no end.** The Father did not make Jesus great at the time of His birth. Christ had been great from all _____.

Percentages

Christ was _____ percent man.

Christ was _____ percent God.

Using heavenly math, those two percentages added together equal _____ percent.

Study a Bible Passage
Matthew 17

Verse 1 **Jesus took . . . Peter and James, and John . . . led them up a high mountain** Jesus's _____ had never upset the three of them before.

Verse 2 **he was transfigured** _____ in form.

his face shone like the sun . . . his clothes became white as light Not only did the face of Jesus radiate glory; His _____ did.

Verse 6 **the disciples . . . fell on their faces and were terrified** The apostles were experiencing _____ and terror toward the glory of Jesus.

Study a Bible Passage
John 17

Verse 1 **Father, the hour has come; glorify your Son** These words, spoken by Jesus, pointed toward the approaching _____ .

the Son may glorify you The Son always desired that any _____ that came to Him would flow to triune God.

Study a Bible Passage
Luke 23

Verse 38 **"This is the King of the Jews."** Jesus was the _____ , and He will be forever and ever.

Student Readers

Reader 1: Therefore, the cross will forever remain the highest evidence of Christ's supremacy—unsurpassed, throughout endless ages. At no point will Jesus ever appear to Christians to be more exalted than when He became the sacrifice for our sin.

Reader 2: Nowhere will He ever blaze forth in victory more vividly than when He was vanquished on Golgotha's tree. To worship Him as He deserves, focused on Him as supreme upon His throne, we must learn first to marvel at Him supreme upon His cross.

QUOTATION

"Christians today appear to know Christ only after the flesh. They try to achieve communion with Him by divesting Him of His burning holiness and unapproachable majesty, the very attributes He veiled while on earth but assumed in fullness of glory upon His ascension to the Father's right hand."

Study a Bible Passage

Ephesians 1

Verse 20 he raised him from the dead and seated him at his right hand in the heavenly places This verse speaks of both the resurrection and the

_____ .

Verse 21 far above . . . every name The Father declared the Son had a _____ above every authority, power, dominion, and name.

Verse 22 put all things under his feet See this quotationi by David Booth.

QUOTATION

"The glory Christ left behind in coming to earth was returned to Him, along with the new glory of all that He victoriously accomplished here. God gave Him the universe's highest place of honor and the highest name of honor, along with the glory of His enemies' humiliation."

Study a Bible Passage

Revelation 1

Verse 10 a loud voice like a trumpet God the Father speaking, about to draw attention to _____ .

Verse 13 son of man The _____ of Christ

clothed with a long robe and with a golden sash around his chest Garments symbolic of the _____

Verse 14 The hairs of his head were white This identifies Christ as _____ .

His eyes were like a flame of fire The _____ of Christ see all and know all.

Verse 15 his voice was like the roar of many waters Christ's voice carries the _____ over the earth.

Verse 17 When I saw him, I fell at his feet as though dead. _____ men are overwhelmed with the glory of Christ.

JESUS AND HEAVEN'S THRONE

Study a Bible Passage

Revelation 5

Verse 11 Then I looked, and I heard around the throne and the living creatures and the elders the voice of many angels Angels and the redeemed from earth praise triune God.

numbering myriads of myriads A number impossible to _____

Verse 12 saying with a loud voice, "Worthy is the Lamb who was slain, to receive power and wealth and wisdom and might and honor and glory and blessing!" _____ terms describe the Lamb.

Verse 13 every creature in heaven and on earth and under the earth and in the sea, and all that is in them, saying, "To him who sits on the throne and to the Lamb _____ and adoration are declared to Christ precisely as to God.

blessing and honor and glory and might forever and ever!" All created beings, all _____ , and all the saints declare glory to the King.

Double Helix

Similar to the double helix of a DNA molecule, Christian worship is the intertwining of _____ and _____ toward King Jesus.

CENTRALITY AND SUPREMACY

Student Readers

Centrality: I am Centrality. I want Jesus to come be the center of what I've got going on.

Supremacy: I am Supremacy. I too want Jesus to come be the center of what I've got going on. But I want so much more. I want to go to King Jesus and become part of what He is doing.

Centrality: I want Jesus to be the center of my life.

Supremacy: That's fine. But which Jesus do you want at the center of your life? A Jesus who's preoccupied with just you and who serves you, or a King who's reigning over the universe?

Centrality: Well, I haven't exactly thought about that.

Supremacy: I want King Jesus at the center of my life, and I want even more than that. I want to be right at the center of Jesus's life.

Centrality: I'm all about Christ's right to be kept at the center of who we are, where we're headed, all we're doing, and how we're blessed.

Supremacy: I agree, but there's so much more. Christ has every right to keep us at the center of who He is, where He's headed, what He's imparting, and how He's blessed.

Your Worship

Write below something you are tempted to worship, even though it pales in comparison to the majestic King of the universe.

_____

_____

_____

_____

_____

Share in Pairs

Person 1: I know Jesus is always with me, but I don't think about Him until I have a problem. It's almost as if He is a little friend in my pocket. When I do have some difficulty, I quickly pull Him out, tell Him my troubles, and then expect Him to fix things the way I want. I assume He's OK with all this since life is really about me.

Person 2: (Help your friend have a more accurate view of the majestic King Jesus.)

JESUS AND THE TRINITY

Student Readers

Leader: What makes God, God? It is the relationship of total and mutual self-giving within triune God.

Father: The Father gives everything to the Son.

Son: The Son offers back all that He has to glorify the Father.

Spirit: And the love of each is sealed by the Holy Spirit.

Father: Every dimension of hope is initiated by the Father . . .

Spirit: . . . developed by the Spirit . . .

Son: . . . while exalting the Son. Ultimately, it is the uniqueness of His relationship to the Father and the Spirit that bestows on the Son preeminence in everything.

Father: Nothing about Christ as the focus of God's promises should ever rob the Father . . .

Spirit: . . . or the Spirit of equal praise.

CHRIST ENTHRONED CHANGES EVERYTHING

What I Wanted

Circle a number below.

One month ago:
1 I wanted everything the world offers and didn't see much need for Jesus.
2 I really wanted Jesus, but at the same time I wanted much the world offers.
3 I wanted Jesus so badly everything else faded in comparison.

Student Readers

Reader 1: In Galatians 2:20, the Bible says, "I have been crucified with Christ. It is no longer I who live, but Christ who lives in me."

Reader 2: Well, if Jesus were just a mascot, I guess it would still be cool to have Him living in me.

Reader 3: But here's what absolutely blows my mind. Jesus obviously is not a mascot. His power and might are beyond understanding. Right this moment He is presiding over the entire universe. The King of all kings actually lives in me. This changes everything!

COUNTING ALL AS LOSS

Study Bible Passages
Colossians 3

Verse 1 **you have been raised with Christ** Desiring what is important to Christ is a direct result of _____ the supreme Ruler of the universe and His _____ the believer.

Verse 2 **Set your minds on things that are above** Priorities look completely different when viewed through   .

Verse 3 **your life is hidden with Christ** The majestic One is   believers, and believers are   His Majesty.

Galatians 2

Verse 20 **It is no longer I who live, but Christ who lives in me.** If a believer dies to self but only invites   to live through him, little is gained. But if a believer   and invites the reigning Monarch of the universe to live through him, then everything is gained.

Colossians 1

Verse 27b **Christ in you, the hope of glory** Intimacy with Christ in His   filling us with expectancy.

Act It Out

Paul: Once I was known as Saul. For a while I made murderous threats against the Lord's disciples. All I could find I put in prison. That's why I was traveling to Damascus.

Christ: Saul, why are you persecuting me?

Paul: Who are you, Lord?

Christ: I am Jesus, whom you are persecuting.

Paul: When I saw the glorified King, I could never be the same. Now I count everything as loss because of the surpassing worth of knowing Christ Jesus my Lord. For His sake I have suffered the loss of all things and count them as rubbish so that I may gain Christ. I am utterly preoccupied with what's on Christ's heart.

Reader: Here's the best part. Counting all loss for His surpassing greatness opens the door for King Jesus to live His powerful life through us. In His strength we will then complete the mission we each have on earth, which will bring great glory to God. And that happens to be the reason for our existence.

COUNT AS LOSS: POSSESSIONS

Study a Bible Passage

Mark 14

Verse 3 **she broke the flask and poured it over his head** Knowing Jesus changed how the women felt about her _____ possession.

Verses 4–5 **Why was the ointment wasted . . . they scolded her** The apostles completely missed the fact that an _____ gift to Jesus never is wasted.

Verse 6 **She has done a beautiful thing to me.** This extravagant _____ revealed the woman's faith in Jesus, her sincere love to Him, and her desire for His honor and glory.

Student Readers

Reader 1: When Zacchaeus was transformed by Christ, one of the stingiest men on the earth suddenly wanted to do something extravagant. He announced, "Behold, Lord, the half of my goods I give to the poor. And if I have defrauded anyone of anything, I restore it fourfold" (Luke 19:8). He probably was dancing around like Ebenezer Scrooge on Christmas morning. Jesus just does that to people.

Reader 2: When you discover the glorious greatness of Christ, responding with acts of extravagance makes perfect sense. He indeed is worthy. Jesus may or may not ask you to give away everything you own. But He calls you and every believer to be willing if He asks.

Reader 1: There is nothing wrong with a popular purse or the best sunshades. As you pray before the throne, sometimes the King might say He wants to bless you with something extra nice.

Reader 2: But other times you may choose to do something extravagant—like giving those same funds to provide school supplies and a backpack for a child overseas. Or to pay for a box of Bibles for a secret church in a closed country. Giving such gifts is delightful when your delight is in the One who has captured your heart.

COUNT AS LOSS: EGO AND FAME

Becoming Famous

On a scale of 1 to 10:
Becoming famous in my life represents a _____.

Before I started this study, my seeing Jesus become more famous in the world would have been a _____.

Student Readers

Reader 1: John the Baptist was the son of a priest. This gave him status. He could have become as famous as his father. Instead he chose to become an anonymous preacher out in the wilderness.

Reader 2: For a while no one knew his name, and he was OK with that. He just kept preaching.

Reader 1: But after some time his reputation began to grow, and the crowds swelled. He was starting to become a big deal. It had to be exciting to see big shots from town in the audience.

Reader 2: But just about the time the crowds were at their peak, Jesus arrived, wanting to be baptized.

Reader 1: John had a clear decision to make: Do I continue enjoying being the center of attention, or do I step into the shadows so all the attention will go to Christ Jesus? His decision was quick, and his announcement was clear.

Hear a Bible Passage
John 1 and 3

"I am not the Christ." . . . "I am the voice of one crying out in the wilderness, 'Make straight the way of the Lord,' as the prophet Isaiah said." . . . "Among you stands one you do not know, even he who comes after me, the strap of whose sandal I am not worthy to untie." . . . "Behold, the Lamb of God, who takes away the sin of the world! This is he of whom I said, 'After me comes a man who ranks before me, because he was before me.' I myself did not know him, but for this purpose I came baptizing with water, that he might be revealed to Israel." . . . **"And I have seen and have borne witness that this is the Son of God"** (John 1:20–34). **"He must increase, but I must decrease"** (John 3:30).

Student Reader

Reader: I must surrender my fascination with myself to a more worthy preoccupation with the character and purposes of Christ. I am not the point. He is. I exist for Him. He does not exist for me.

COUNT AS LOSS: RELATIONSHIPS

Hear a Bible Passage

2 Corinthians 11:24–27

Five times I received at the hands of the Jews the forty lashes less one. Three times I was beaten with rods. Once I was stoned. Three times I was shipwrecked; a night and a day I was adrift at sea; on frequent journeys, in danger from rivers, danger from robbers, danger from my own people, danger from Gentiles, danger in the city, danger in the wilderness, danger at sea, danger from false brothers; in toil and hardship, through many a sleepless night, in hunger and thirst, often without food, in cold and exposure.

A Prayer Paul *Didn't* Pray

"Lord Jesus, I love this. Finally, people are nice to me. I want to become the permanent pastor of these people. I know you mentioned leaving and going through more hard times, but I think that's a bad plan. I'm ready for a little me time. I will serve You—but here—my way—with my new friends."

Hear a Bible Passage

Acts 20:22–25

And now, behold, I am going to Jerusalem, constrained by the Spirit, not knowing what will happen to me there, except that the Holy Spirit testifies to me in every city that imprisonment and afflictions await me. But I do not account my life of any value nor as precious to myself, if only I may finish my course and the ministry that I received from the Lord Jesus, to testify to the gospel of the grace of God. And now, behold, I know that none of you among whom I have gone about proclaiming the kingdom will see my face again.

Student Readers

Reader 1: You have seen soldiers tearfully saying goodbye to family and friends.

Reader 2: You have seen sailors looking longingly to those they love as their ship pulls out. Leaving is tough, no doubt about it.

Reader 1: But here's a key question: Is it right for members of the military to leave those they love for a season to protect the nation?

Reader 2: An earthly nation matters, but a heavenly kingdom matters much more.

Reader 1: If eighteen-year-olds leave close friends to protect democracy, then it makes perfect sense for eighteen-year-olds to leave close friends to take the gospel to the ends of the earth.

COUNT AS LOSS: A LONG LIFE

Study Bible Passages

Acts 6

Verses 8–9 And Stephen, full of grace and power, was doing great wonders . . . disputed with Stephen The _____ were furious at Stephen for proclaiming that Jesus was the Son of God.

Verses 12–13 brought him before the council . . . and they set up false witnesses Stephen's "trial" was just as _____ and as Jesus's.

Acts 7

Verse 54 they were enraged When people deep inside know they are doing bad things, they tend to _____ when they hear the truth.

Verse 55 he . . . saw . . . Jesus standing at the right hand of God.

Verse 56 And he said, "Behold, I see the heavens opened, and the Son of Man standing at the right hand of God." Seeing Jesus _____ was all Stephen needed.

Verses 57–58 they cast him out of the city and stoned him The leaders forgot the pretense of a _____ and just began stoning Stephen to death.

Summary

Stephen must have thought, *My King is watching and He knows. This act is for Him!*

Questions for Silent Reflection

Would you lay down your life to remain true and faithful to your Monarch?

Would you also boldly live for King Jesus in front of your peers?

Which of the two takes more courage?

COUNT AS LOSS: EVERYTHING

Student Readers

Reader 1: Do you believe Christ has just called you to be a nice church member? Or do you believe He has called you to be His disciple?

Reader 2: Has He called you just to be religious? Or has He called you to go all-in with Him—live or die?

Reader 1: Listen carefully how Christ defines the call to be a disciple:

Reader 2: "If anyone would come after me, let him deny himself and take up his cross and follow me. For whoever would save his life will lose it, but whoever loses his life for my sake and the gospel's will save it" (Mark 8:34–35).

Reader 1: "Whoever loves father or mother more than me is not worthy of me, and whoever loves son or daughter more than me is not worthy of me" (Matt. 10:37).

Reader 2: Why would anyone go all-in for Jesus? Why would anyone choose to be His disciple? The short answer is, He is worthy of that. The Lamb on the throne of heaven absolutely is worthy.

Reader 1: So, what is His perspective on millions of people who want only a little Jesus? Who want only a little friend in their pocket?

Reader 2: Jesus says such a person "cannot be my disciple" (Luke 14:26, 27, 33).

Study a Bible Passage

Mark 10

Verses 28–30 we have left everything and followed you. . . . no one who has left house or brothers or sisters or mother or father or children or lands, for my sake and for the gospel, who will not receive a hundredfold now . . . and in the age to come eternal life. Christ has a clear plan to rectify all   in the age to come.

Verse 31 many who are first will be last, and the last first What believers   on earth is temporary. What Christ blesses believers with on New Earth they will have   .

The Columbine High School Shooting

On April 20, 1999, two students at Columbine High School killed twelve classmates and one teacher. The *Boston Globe* carried this report four days later.

"'Do you believe in God,' one of the heavily armed gunmen asked the shy blond girl reading her Bible in the library while her school was under siege. 'Yes, I believe in God,' she replied in a voice strong enough to be heard by classmates cowering under nearby tables and desks.

"The gunman in the long black trench coat laughed. 'Why?' he asked mockingly. Then he raised his gun and shot and killed seventeen-year-old Cassie Bernall. Accounts of the final moments of Cassie's life echo with the history of early Christendom, when a profession of faith could be a fatal act."

The day after the shooting, her brother Chris found on Cassie's desk a poem she wrote after church services the Sunday before. She must have been reading Philippians 3.

> *Now I have given up on everything else—*
> *I have found it to be the only way to really know*
> *Christ and to experience the*
> *mighty power that brought*
> *him back to life again, and to find*
> *out what it means to suffer and to*
> *die with him. So, whatever it takes*
> *I will be one who lives in the fresh*
> *newness of life of those who are*
> *alive from the dead.*

WAKING UP THE WORLD TO CHRIST

Student Readers

Reader 1: Only by the grace of God, we're on our way to becoming Christ-driven Christians. Even more than before, we're committed to Christ Himself. He sets the devotion, the direction, and the destiny for our lives.

Reader 2: But here's the question: Is this awakening to more of Christ just supposed to be for us? Or would that mean going back to a me-centered faith? Wouldn't a faith that's all about me be the opposite of a true Christ awakening?

Reader 1: You've nailed the issue. To whom much is given much is required. In the power of the Spirit, the Father wants us to join Him in waking up others to the glory of His Son. We can become infectious advocates of Christ awakenings wherever we go.

Fill in Blanks

A deficient _____ for Christ's glory plagues many churches.

A loss of _____ in Christ's glory exhausts many churches.

A loss of _____ toward Christ's glory weakens many churches.

A diminished _____ of Christ's glory impoverishes many churches.

Discuss in Pairs

1. Do I personally know Christ well enough to present Him to other Christians fully enough to help them come back to Him for all He is?

2. Have I ever offered myself to the Father for this primary purpose: to be reawakened by His Spirit to the greater glory of His Son so I can invite other believers to embrace Christ's supremacy?

AWAKEN BELIEVERS TO THE GREATNESS OF JESUS

Study Bible Passages

Colossians 1

Verse 25 make the word of God fully known Paul wanted new believers and seasoned believers to grasp   that Christ really is.

Verse 28 that we may present everyone mature in Christ Paul was focused on waking up the   to the majestic Son of God.

Colossians 3

Verse 16 teaching and admonishing one another Paul challenged believers to have   about Christ whenever they come together.

Fill in Blanks

                Christ proclaimers make Christ and His supremacy their primary message.

                Christ proclaimers pray that their conversations will help reintroduce believers to Christ and His supremacy.

                Christ proclaimers study and teach God's Word as a book that reveals much more of Christ.

                Christ proclaimers give Christ daily obedience.

                Christ proclaimers have no desire to promote themselves.

                Christ proclaimers help believers interpret every element of life from the perspective of Christ's all-encompassing reign.

                Christ proclaimers are caregivers sent to believers in the grip of despair to bring a fresh vision of Jesus's glory.

Discussion Questions

Which of the characteristics above sound like you?

Where do you want to grow?

Choose Numbers

Before this study, I was motivated to share with friends and other believers what I'm learning about Christ—to share with them the fresh insights into His greatness and glory I was uncovering.

On a scale of 1 to 10, I was a _____. *(1 = zero motivated; 10 = totally motivated)*

Now I'm motivated to share with friends and other believers what I'm learning about Christ—to share with them fresh insights into His greatness and glory I'm uncovering.

On a scale of 1 to 10, I am a _____. *(1 = zero motivated; 10 = totally motivated)*

Before this study, I encouraged other believers to talk with me about their discoveries regarding the wonders of who Jesus really is.

On a scale of 1 to 10, I was a _____. *(1 = I never did; 10 = I continually did)*

Now I want to encourage other believers to talk with me about their discoveries regarding the wonders of who Jesus really is.

On a scale of 1 to 10, I am a _____. *(1 = zero motivated; 10 = totally motivated)*

Discussion Questions

If you are to be a disciple who makes disciples, then what is at the heart of that process?

Can you think of any part of disciple making more important than awakening the person you are discipling to the glory of King Jesus?

Unison Reading

Leader: I challenge you to follow the leadership of God the Father in the power of God the Spirit. Then, with humility and gratitude, each evening you will be able to say:

Students:
I know that this day
my life has counted
for Christ and His kingdom,
by proclaiming the hope of His supremacy,
calling my generation to
awake to Christ for all He is.

Leader: For the whole church to take the whole gospel to the whole world, we must restore the whole vision of God's Son among God's people.

TELL THE LOST

Study Bible Passages

John 14

Verse 15 **"If you love me, you will keep my commandments."** Chief among Christ's _____ is found in Matthew 28:18–20.

Matthew 28

Verses 18–19 **Go therefore and make disciples of all nations**
Verse 20 **teaching them to observe all that I have commanded you.** Passion for Jesus's supremacy motivates believers to share Him and His gospel with those who are lost, doing so in such a way as to exalt His _____, spread His _____, and extend His _____ before them.

Student Readers

Reader 1: Listen to these words from David Bryant. "World evangelization is about the Father multiplying communities across the globe, raised up by the power of the Spirit, marked by adoration for and wholehearted obedience to the Son, as we hasten toward the day when all of heaven and earth will be filled forever with numberless lovers and worshippers of the Lamb on the throne."

Reader 2: Listen to these words from John Piper. "The greatest cause in the world is joyfully rescuing people from hell, meeting their earthly needs, making them glad in God, and doing it with a kind, serious pleasure that makes Christ look like the treasure that he is. No war on earth was ever fought for a greater cause or a greater king."

Reader 3: Listen to these words from David Platt. "You have a choice. You can cling to short-term treasures that you cannot keep, or you can live for long-term treasures that you cannot lose: people coming to Christ; men, women, and children living because they now have food; unreached tribes receiving the gospel. And the all-consuming satisfaction of knowing and experiencing Christ as the treasure above all others."

Powerful Thought

A true disciple says to Jesus, "My answer is yes. Now where do You want me to go?"

LOOK FORWARD TO HEAVEN

Hear a Bible Passage
Revelation 22:3–5

Reader 1: No longer will there be anything accursed, but the throne of God and of the Lamb will be in it, and his servants will worship him.

Reader 2: They will see his face, and his name will be on their foreheads.

Reader 1: And night will be no more. They will need no light of lamp or sun, for the Lord God will be their light, and they will reign forever and ever.

Study a Bible Passage
Ephesians 1

Verses 16–18 **having the eyes of your hearts enlightened** Paul was praying that believers' minds might understand the _____ that awaited them.

that you may know what is the hope Paul wanted believers to know the hope of the glorious _____ that is theirs.

Verses 19–20 **he worked in Christ when he raised him from the dead and seated him at his right hand** God's promises are made solid by the resurrection, ascension, and _____ of King Jesus.

Ted Dekker said, "But I say with Paul, fix your mind on heaven. Fascinate your mind with Christ, and fan into flames a vision of the afterlife. Obsess after the bliss that awaits you as a joint heir with Christ in heaven."

Student Readers

Reader 1: Ted Dekker said, "With the Lord we love and with the friends we cherish, believers will embark together on the ultimate adventure, in a spectacular new universe awaiting our dominion and exploration. Jesus will be the cosmic center. Joy will be the air we breathe."

Reader 2: David Bryant said, "The Consummation will inaugurate an unprecedented fellowship. Earth will be filled with exultant saints from all the ages, ready to become dearest neighbors forever. The Bible teaches that history's final chapter will introduce one single, world-sized society, comprised of people from every tongue and nation."

FINAL COMMITMENT

Student Readers

Reader 1: Listen as we describe a life fully awakened to King Jesus. We challenge you to . . .

Reader 2: See Jesus more fully for all He is by how you study about Him throughout God's Word—which leads you to . . .

Reader 3: Seek Jesus more fully for all He is by how you pursue and encounter Him through prayer—which leads you to . . .

Reader 4: Savor Jesus more fully for all He is by how you praise Him through worship—which leads you to . . .

Reader 1: Speak of Jesus more fully for all He is by how you talk about Him with believers—which leads you to . . .

Reader 2: Show Jesus more fully for all He is by how you imitate Him in word and deed—which leads you to . . .

Reader 3: Serve Jesus more fully for all He is by how you minister to others for His sake—which leads you to . . .

Reader 4: Share with Jesus more fully for all He is by how you introduce unbelievers to Him as Lord and Savior.

Two Challenges

Adult Reader: David Bryant said, "We follow a Master who marched out of a graveyard to ascend the Throne of the Universe. . . . A comprehensive vision of the supremacy of Christ will always lead to a consuming passion for Christ. ... Will passion for Christ's supremacy become the driving motivation of your life?"

Student Reader: Teenage author Jaquelle Crowe said, "Be humble, be wonderstruck, be faithful, and throw yourself into a single-focused pursuit of this King of the universe. Take up your cross, deny yourself daily, and follow him. God is at work in this generation. He's raising up young people to reject the status quo and risk everything to obey him. That's our generation. That's me. That's you. And this is our calling."

Journal

New Thoughts about the Majesty of Christ

Look forward to even more insights in how you see Christ as you absorb more and more of His Word, the Bible.

Proclamation

Sovereign Son of the Father, reigning at His right hand forever and ever!

Triumphant Victor over every foe—sin, death, and hades!

Glorious Conqueror, the dominating personality for all ages to come!

Supreme Commander of heaven's hosts, ready to obey Your every word!

Righteous Judge of peoples and nations, to whom all must give an account!

Undeniable Ruler of history, overseeing its outcome from beginning to end!

Incomparable King of an empire that will fill creation with Your power!

Only Head of a people whom You have bought with Your own blood!

Reigning Redeemer, sending Your salvation to the ends of the earth!

Supreme Lord now just as fully as You will be at the end of time!

Amen!

LITTLE JESUS IN MY POCKET

What is the most frequently used word in the following lines?

Jesus came into the world for me.
He will always be there for me,
constantly available to me,
as a ready resource for me,
ensuring maximum happiness for me,
always ready to respond to me,
to protect and deliver me,
to fulfill all that concerns me.

Those lines raise an interesting question. Is your faith about Jesus or mostly about you?

How does the following prayer sound like you? How does the prayer sound very different from you?

> *Jesus, I know there are things in the Bible that I don't know. And I know there are some complicated things our church teaches that I don't understand. But I used to think, "At least I understand Jesus. I may not grasp everything, but at least I pretty much understand my Savior." But right now, I'm not so sure.*
>
> *Granted, I do understand a lot about You. I absolutely believe You are God. And I'm certain Your death on the cross paid the price for my sin. I have total faith that I belong to You and that You will take me to heaven when I die. All those things I have believed with all my heart.*

*But here's what I'm starting to figure out. You've been
important to me mostly because of the good things
You've brought to me. As I think about my prayers over
the past few months, mostly I've been asking You to do
things for me and for people important to me. I hate to
admit it, but I've wanted Your presents more than Your
presence.*

*I'm not sure You've really been on my mind that much,
except for when I've needed something from You. It's not
that I do a lot of terrible things. It's just that I pretty much
live my life the way I want to. Most of the time I want
what's best for me, so I just try to make that happen. As
I move through the day, I guess You're not really on my
mind very much at all. It makes me sad to say that.*

*But I want You to know I'm ready for a change. I want to
figure out much more about who You really are today.
Yes, You are my friend, and You always will be. But now
I can tell You are much more than that. You are the King
over everything! And I have a hunch that fact is about to
turn my life upside down. I'm excited to know the real You.
Thanks for being patient until I could come to this day.
I think this is the start of a great new adventure. In Your
name, Amen.*

Read Revelation 3:14–21

King Jesus spoke to seven churches in Revelation 2–3. The final church
He addressed was the church in Laodicea. The book of Revelation was
written years after Jesus had ascended back to heaven. By this time the
Laodicean church had forgotten that Christ is King.

Instead of living under the kingship of Christ, the church members had
become preoccupied with themselves. They were proud that their
famous garment industry brought wealth into the city. Perhaps that
is why Jesus pointed out that spiritually they were naked (see verses
17–18). Also, the people were proud that their city produced a famous
ointment for the eyes. That may have caused Jesus to point out their
spiritual blindness.

Then, Jesus says something remarkable in verse 20: "Behold, I stand at the door and knock. If anyone hears my voice and opens the door, I will come in to him and eat with him, and he with me." Jesus said this to the Laodicean church. He was speaking to believers. They had lost so much focus on King Jesus that He now saw Himself standing outside His own church!

Since He possesses all the power in the universe, Jesus could have forced the Laodiceans to relate to Him as King. Instead He granted them the privilege of making that decision for themselves.

Today He is doing the same thing. He approaches believers who are preoccupied with themselves, He knocks on the door of their hearts, and He invites them to embrace Him as King. King Jesus has big plans for those who kneel before Him as King and who join Him in bringing His kingdom on earth. Jesus says, "The one who conquers, I will grant him to sit with me on my throne, as I also conquered and sat down with my Father on his throne" (Rev. 3:21).

Are you ready to open the door?

Pray

Consider using the letters A.C.T.S. as an outline for prayer.

Adoration—tell Christ many ways you adore Him and find Him glorious.

Confession—agree with Christ that sin is sin and embrace the forgiveness He won for you on the cross.

Thanksgiving—tell Christ many different ways you are thankful for who He is and what He has done.

Supplication—pray for others and pray for yourself. Pray primarily that Christ will give you ways to join Him to bring His kingdom on earth for His glory.

Lord Christ, joyfully I open the door of my heart to You and kneel before You. I so love You and adore You. Mighty King, You do not exist for me. I exist for You and Your kingdom. Holy Spirit of God, across these next three studies, reveal to me much more of who the Son truly is, for the glory of God. Amen.

SPEAKER NOTES

WHO JESUS IS TODAY

How You See Jesus = How You See God

Christian leader David Bryant said, "What you think (and are able to share) about God's Son is the single most important thing anyone can know about you." That statement is true for several reasons, but here's one of the most important: a believer's view of Jesus becomes the believer's view of God.

God is one, but He exists in three persons. God the Father, God the Son, and God the Holy Spirit make up the Trinity or triune God. Today, God the Son is the clearest revelation of who triune God is. Notice what the Bible says.

Read Hebrews 1:1–3 (emphasis added)

"Long ago, at many times and in many ways, God spoke to our fathers by the prophets, but in these last days he has spoken to us by his Son . . . [The Son] is the radiance of the glory of God and the *exact imprint* of his nature."

Read Colossians 1:15

"[The Son] is the image of the invisible God."

How a believer sees Jesus will be how a believer sees God. A little Jesus becomes a little God. A mascot Jesus becomes a mascot God. Needless to say, this is a huge issue.

When You Go to Heaven

No one knows exactly how things will be in heaven, so use your imagination. Imagine that you die unexpectedly and moments later you arrive in heaven. Similar to a welcoming committee, those you were closest to on earth are there to greet you. Even while you're hugging necks, the others notice you're dazzled by the beauty of heaven. They smile and say, "Oh, you haven't seen anything yet. Come on, you've got to see King Jesus!"

As you and the others laugh and walk, you notice the music is getting louder and louder. In addition to the music, you also hear two booming voices that make the ground shake. The voices repeat "Holy, holy, holy is the Lord God Almighty."

Then you turn a corner and you see Him. Seated at the right hand of the Father is King Jesus! You have to strain your neck to look up into His loving and radiant face. But then something astonishing happens. His kind and fiery eyes look down at you. With a voice that reverberates through heaven, He says, "Speak to Me, my child."

In that moment, what are you going to say to Him? What will you say to the powerful and majestic King over the entire universe?

Write the first sentences you would say.

Before You Go to Heaven

Are you trusting Christ alone for the forgiveness of your sins and for life in heaven with Him? If so, then you *will* stand before Him on His throne, and you *will* speak to Him there. But here is an amazing thought. *Right now* Christ is on the throne. *Right now* He invites you to speak to Him. What will you say to the King of glory? Would you like to speak the following lines to Him as part of your prayer of praise?

"Yours, O LORD, is the greatness and the power and the glory and the victory and the majesty, for all that is in the heavens and in the earth is yours. Yours is the kingdom, O LORD, and you are exalted as head above all" (1 Chron. 29:11).

"To the King of ages, immortal, invisible, the only God, be honor and glory forever and ever. Amen" (1 Tim. 1:17).

"Now to him who is able to keep you from stumbling and to present you blameless before the presence of his glory with great joy, to the only God, our Savior, through Jesus Christ our Lord, be glory, majesty, dominion, and authority, before all time and now and forever. Amen" (Jude 24–25).

"To him who sits on the throne and to the Lamb be blessing and honor and glory and might forever and ever!" (Rev. 5:13).

Forever

Today you can speak to Jesus with all the awe, respect, and wonder a King deserves. And you can speak to Him with the warmth, love, and intimacy He intended when He created you. Here is the best part: the way you speak with Him today is the way you can speak to Him forever!

Pray it

Adoration, Confession, Thanksgiving, Supplication for Others, then—

Lord Christ, I so love You and adore You. Holy Spirit of God, bless You and thank You for revealing to me more of who the Son is today. King Jesus, I am thrilled with my new way of seeing You and approaching You and speaking to You. I never, ever want to go back to a small way of seeing You. Your voice, Your truth, Your ways, and Your glory transcend all others. I belong to Your kingdom both now and for eternity. In Your mighty name, Amen.

SPEAKER NOTES

CHRIST ENTHRONED CHANGES EVERYTHING

Enthroned King Jesus appeared to Paul on the road to Damascus. Christ's glory was so great it blinded Paul for a few days. Later Paul would write, "I count everything as loss because of the surpassing worth of knowing Christ Jesus my Lord" (Phil. 3:8).

Notice what Paul did *not* say. He did not say, "I count everything as loss because my religion told me I had to." He did not say, "I count everything as loss because the church has rules and that is one of the big rules." For Paul, "I want to" was a much, much stronger motivation than "I have to."

Christ does have every right to claim authority over us. David Booth summarizes five reasons that is true:

1. He created us for Himself. "Everyone who is called by my name, whom I created for my glory, whom I formed and made" (Isa. 43:7).

2. He purchased us with His blood. "[Jesus] died for all, that those who live might no longer live for themselves but for him who for their sake died and was raised" (2 Cor. 5:15).

3. His resurrection gave us life. "Jesus said to her, 'I am the resurrection and the life. Whoever believes in me, though he die, yet shall he live'" (John 11:25).

4. He pursued us for adoption. "For you did not receive the spirit of slavery to fall back into fear, but you have received the Spirit of adoption as sons, by whom we cry, 'Abba! Father!'" (Rom. 8:15).

5. He chose us for permanent union. "The one who conquers, I will grant him to sit with me on my throne, as I also conquered and sat down with my Father on his throne" (Rev. 3:21).

Paul understood, perhaps better than anyone, those five factors. He spoke to each factor in the letters he wrote. And yet Paul considered everything in his life as loss *primarily* because of the surpassing greatness of Christ Himself. Paul believed the Son of God is worthy to receive from us our highest worship, most fervent love, and complete surrender. Perhaps you agree.

Pray

Consider pausing right now to declare praise to King Jesus.

We behold You and rejoice in You as the triumphant Lamb before whom all creation and all the redeemed of all the ages bow down and worship, before whom all of us here and now bow down and worship. To You belong blessing and honor and glory and strength and power forever and ever. All of Scripture, all of creation, all of history, all of the purposes and prophecies and promises of God are summed up in You alone.

You

Are you prepared to consider all as loss compared to the present greatness of Christ? Compared to Him, would you count as loss . . .
  Your present and future possessions . . .
   Your ego and fame . . .
    Your relationships . . .
     Your comfort and long life?

Here's the best part. Counting all loss for His surpassing greatness opens the door for Christ to live His powerful life through us. In His strength we will then complete the mission we each have on earth, which will bring great glory to God. And that happens to be the reason for our existence.

Pray

Adoration, Confession, Thanksgiving, Supplication for Others, then—

Lord Christ, I so love You and adore You. I embrace You far, far more than I embrace my immediate world and culture. I love Your world, but my citizenship is not here. I belong to Your kingdom both now and for eternity. Your voice, Your truth, Your ways, and Your glory transcend all others. In Your mighty name, Amen.

Lord Christ, I acknowledge I want more things, and I want to hold onto what I already have. But I am falling more in love with You every day. Increasingly You become more important, and possessions become less important. I delight in counting all things loss for Your surpassing greatness. Reveal to me each time You want me to dedicate some of my possessions to Your kingdom activity.

Lord Christ, if You choose to place me in very visible roles, overwhelm me with Your greatness so I will be moved to deflect any attention coming to me to You. If You choose to place me in background roles, give me such delight in You that I do not need applause. Each day make Your fame more my passion and my fame less so.

Lord Christ, You designed me for relationships, and You are blessing me with relationships today. But my relationship with You transcends all others. For Your great glory and to see Your name become even more famous on the earth, I will release relationships if necessary to follow Your call. I will look forward to an eternity with all those I have loved on the earth.

Lord Christ, You do not exist for me. I exist for You and for Your great glory. It is my high honor and privilege to make any sacrifice necessary to follow Your clear call—including my very life. Though it is unlikely You would call me to lay down my life for the sake of the gospel, I want You to know I would consider it a high honor to do so.

I rest in knowing that if You call me to do hard things, You will give me the courage and strength I will need—right on time. Compared to Your surpassing greatness, I count everything as loss. For the sake of Your name. Amen.

SPEAKER NOTES

WAKING UP THE WORLD TO CHRIST

Think about it! Someday you are going to see this very scene with *your own eyes*:

> *"Then I looked, and I heard around the throne and the living creatures and the elders the voice of many angels, numbering myriads of myriads and thousands of thousands, saying with a loud voice, 'Worthy is the Lamb who was slain, to receive power and wealth and wisdom and might and honor and glory and blessing!' And I heard every creature in heaven and on earth and under the earth and in the sea, and all that is in them, saying, 'To him who sits on the throne and to the Lamb be blessing and honor and glory and might forever and ever!'" (Rev. 5:11–13).*

But what about today, while you still are on earth?

Use your imagination. At the beginning of the day, your King rides up to you on a beautiful white horse. With a flashing smile and unbounded enthusiasm, He calls you to go with Him on great (and sometimes dangerous) adventures. Ego, fame, and fortune can never compare with the thrill of riding off with Him to change the world.

Here's one of the adventures the King has for you: He invites you to wake up other believers to His greatness and glory. Nothing is more strategic for the advance of the kingdom of God's Son than to promote a vision for the full extent of Christ's lordship among believers. How will you speak about the Savior to believers you will be with this Sunday?

A grand vision of who Christ is today is contagious. Think back to the weeks before you began this study. How did you think about Jesus?

How did you see Him and speak to Him? Through the study of Scripture, would you say you now have been "infected" with an expanded view of His power and glory? If so, then it's time to consider how you will join the Spirit in "infecting" others with what you have received.

Many Christians have a me-centered faith right now. But you and your generation can launch an "epidemic" in the church, drawing multitudes of believers into a Christ awakening. For some that awakening will be so dramatic it will almost be like meeting Him for the first time.

Here's a second adventure the King has for you: if many Christians need a grander way of seeing Jesus, then those who are spiritually lost certainly do. Your own awakening to King Jesus is exactly what they need. That is true for those close by and for those all over the world. The will of God is for you to give your life to making the gospel and the glory of the Son known among all peoples, particularly those who have never even heard of Jesus.

In the process of reaching out to unbelievers, the surprising reward will be how Jesus becomes even more precious to you as a result. It's like when a bride-to-be eagerly reports to all her girlfriends what a wonderful man her future husband is to her. To her amazement the very act of sharing him with others ends up deepening her own longings and passions for him as well.

You may get to see the second coming of Christ. When the King descends to be glorified before His saints, all who have believed in Him will marvel (2 Thess. 1:10). But for those who do not belong to Jesus, His arrival will bring panic and fear.

"Then the kings of the earth and the great ones and the generals and the rich and the powerful, and everyone, slave and free, hid themselves in the caves and among the rocks of the mountains, calling to the mountains and rocks, 'Fall on us and hide us from the face of him who is seated on the throne, and from the wrath of the Lamb, for the great day of their wrath has come, and who can stand?'" (Rev. 6:15–17).

In the power of the Spirit, King Jesus is multiplying the number of those who will welcome Him in joy rather than fear. Joining Him in that quest is the adventure of a lifetime.

This study will soon end, but your adventures with
King Jesus are just beginning. . . .

Pray
Adoration, Confession, Thanksgiving, Supplication for Others, then—

*Lord Christ, I so love You and adore You. I embrace my new way of
seeing You and approaching You and speaking to You. I never, ever
want to go back to a small way of seeing You.*

*In the power of the Spirit and for the glory of the Father, I dedicate
myself to waking up other believers to much more of the majesty and
glory of who the Son really is today. And I dedicate myself to introducing
the lost to my supremely wonderful King. Amen.*

SPEAKER NOTES

MORE SCRIPTURES ABOUT THE
GREATNESS OF GOD'S SON

Christ's Supremacy Foreshadowed

Isaiah 9:6–7
Isaiah 42:1–4
Jeremiah 33:15–16
Micah 5:2–4
Zechariah 9:9–11
Psalm 2:6–8
Psalm 21:1–5

Christ's Supremacy Fulfilled

Acts 2:32–36
Romans 8:32–35
1 Corinthians 15:20–26
Ephesians 1:9–10
Philippians 2:9–11
Colossians 1:17–20
2 Thessalonians 1:7–10
Revelation 11:15
John 1:14–16

MY DISCOVERIES ABOUT THE
GREATNESS OF GOD'S SON

MY PRAYERS